How Toys Work

Ramps and Wedges

Siân Smith

Heinemann
LIBRARY

Chicago, Illinois

www.capstonepub.com
Visit our website to find out
more information about
Heinemann-Raintree books.

To order:

☎ Phone 800-747-4992

▭ Visit www.capstonepub.com
to browse our catalog and order online.

Edited by Dan Nunn, Rebecca Rissman, and Sian Smith
Designed by Joanna Hinton-Malivoire
Picture research by Mica Brancic
Production by Victoria Fitzgerald

Originated by Capstone Global Library Ltd

Library of Congress Cataloging-in-Publication Data
Smith, Siân.
  Ramps and wedges / Sian Smith.—1st ed.
    p. cm.—(How toys work)
  Includes bibliographical references and index.
  ISBN 978-1-4329-6581-5 (hb)—ISBN 978-1-4329-6588-4
(pb) 1. Inclined planes—Juvenile literature. 2. Wedges—Juvenile
literature. 3. Toys—Experiments—Juvenile literature. I. Title.
  TJ147.S635 2013
  621.8—dc23   2011041310

Acknowledgments
The author and publisher are grateful to the following for
permission to reproduce copyright material: © Capstone
Publishers pp. 5, 6, 8, 9, 10, 11, 12, 13, 15, 16, 20, 21, 23 middle
bottom (Karon Dubke); Shutterstock pp.4 (© aquariagirl1970),
4 (© charles taylor), 4 (© Fesus Robert), 4 (© Phiseksit), 7 (© LIN,
CHUN-TSO), 18 (© joingate), 19 (© Mike Flippo), 17 inset (©
Daniel Taeger), 17 main (© SeDmi), 22 bottom left (© Mark Yuill),
22 bottom right (© Jiri Vaclavek), 22 top left (© c.byatt-norman),
22 top right (© macka), 22 middle top (© sarah2), 23 top
(© SeDmi).

Cover photograph of a skater reproduced with permission of Getty
Images (Photonica/Connor Walberg). Back cover photograph of
a toy car on a ramp reproduced with permission of © Capstone
Publishers (Karon Dubke).

We would like to thank David Harrison, Nancy Harris, Dee Reid,
and Diana Bentley for their assistance in the preparation of
this book.

Every effort has been made to contact copyright holders of
material reproduced in this book. Any omissions will be rectified in
subsequent printings if notice is given to the publisher.

All the Internet addresses (URLs) given in this book were valid
at the time of going to press. However, due to the dynamic
nature of the Internet, some addresses may have changed, or
sites may have changed or ceased to exist since publication.
While the author and publisher regret any inconvenience this
may cause readers, no responsibility for any such changes can
be accepted by either the author or the publisher.

Contents

Different Toys

There are many different kinds of toys.

Toys work in different ways.

Ramps

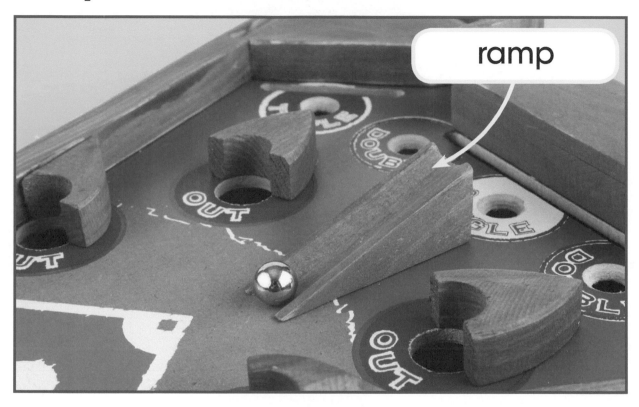

ramp

Some toys use ramps.

side of a hill

A ramp is like the side of a hill.

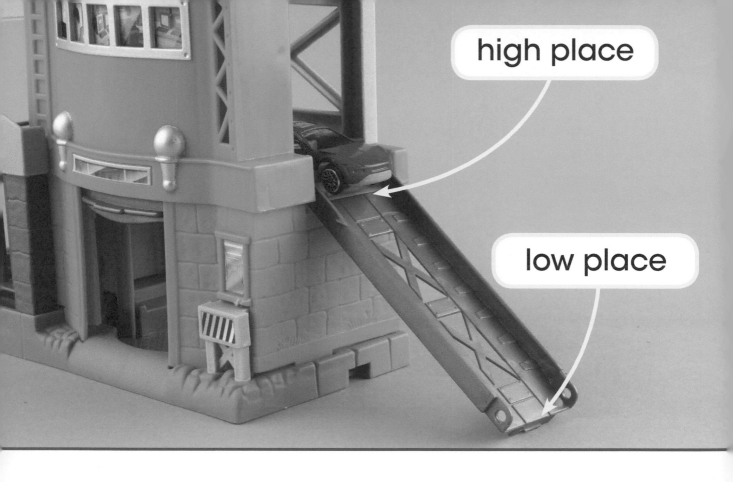

high place

low place

A ramp connects a high place and a low place.

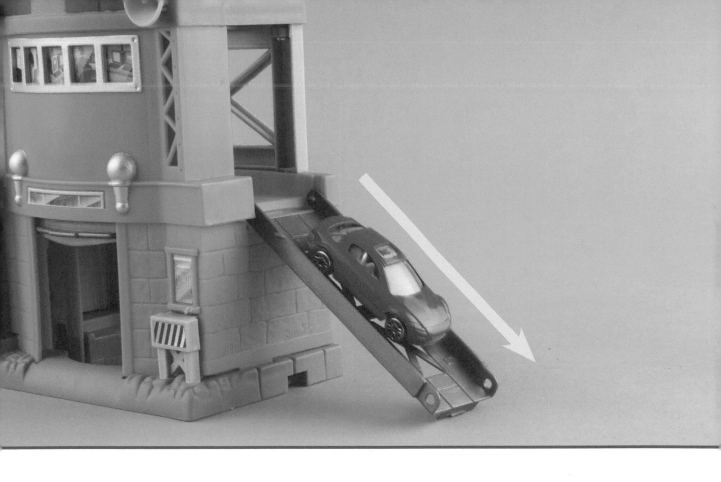

Things can move up or down ramps.

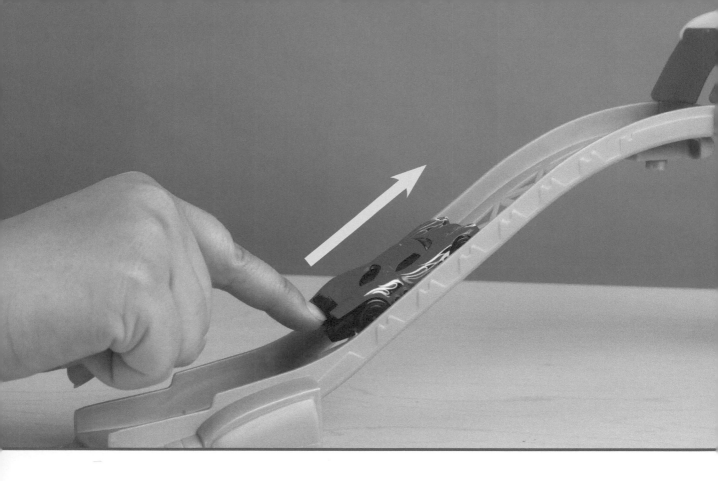

Things can move slowly when they are pushed up a ramp.

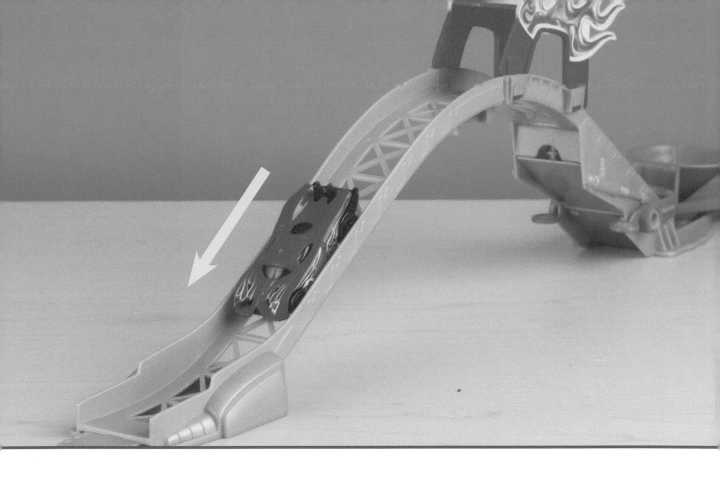

Things can move quickly when they are pushed down a ramp.

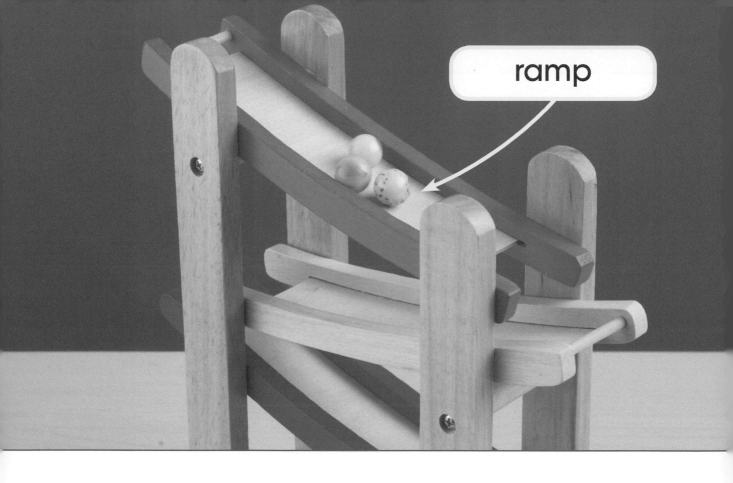

ramp

This marble run is a ramp.

This slide is a ramp.

Wedges

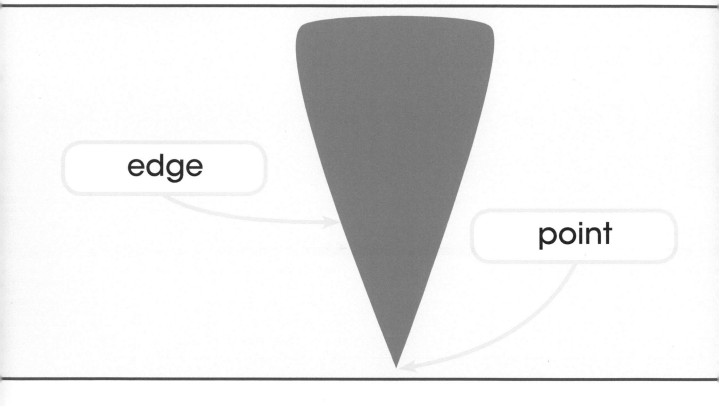

edge

point

A wedge has a sharp edge or point.

wedge

We can push wedges into things.

Wedges can stop things from moving.

wedge

Wedges can cut things apart.

wedge

The end of this shovel is a wedge.

It pushes the sand apart.

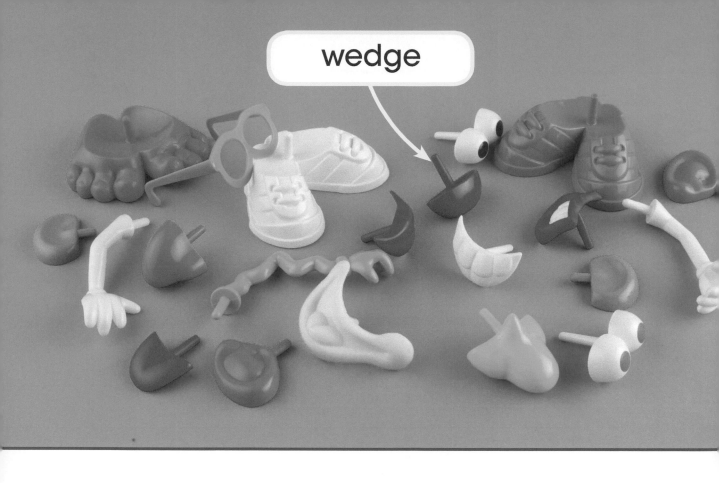

wedge

These toys have wedges.

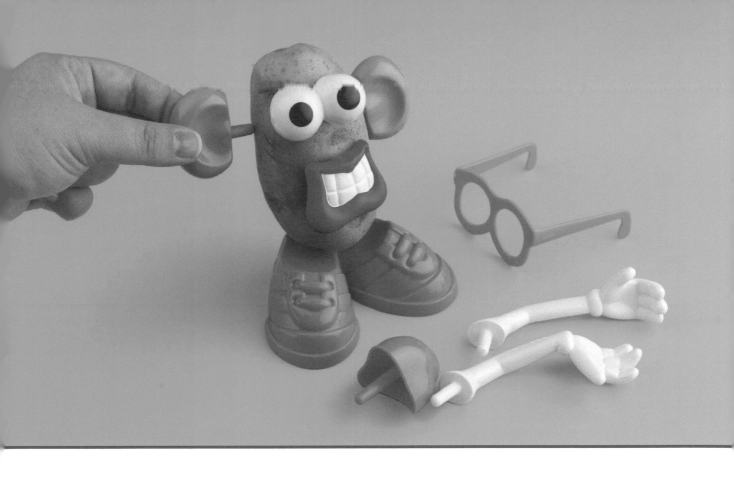

You push them into the potato.

Quiz

a

b

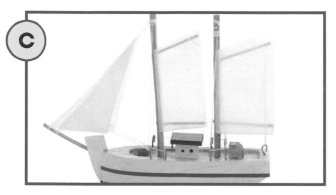

c

d

Which one of these toys uses a wedge to work?

Answer on page 24

Picture Glossary

 **edge** side of something. Some edges can be sharp.

 **point** sharp end. The end of a dart is a point.

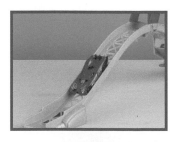 **ramp** a ramp is like a slope. It connects a high place and a low place.

 **wedge** piece of hard material with a sharp edge or point

Index

Answer to question on page 22:
Toy b uses a wedge to work. A nail is a wedge.

Notes for Parents and Teachers

Introduce ramps

Show an example of a simple ramp. Explain that a ramp is like a slope that connects a low place and a high place. (Ramps are also called inclined planes.) It is easier to move something heavy from a low place to a high place if you use a ramp. Help the children to design and carry out an investigation using ramps. For example, investigate how far a toy car will travel if given a small push or big push down a ramp, or how changing the steepness of the ramp affects the distance it travels.

Introduce wedges

Show the children an example of a wedge—for instance, a plastic knife. Explain that wedges have at least one slanting side that ends in a sharp edge. We push wedges into things to split them apart. Knives, forks, axes, and scissor blades are examples of wedges. We also sometimes use wedges to keep two things separate and to stop them from moving.

Follow-up activities

Take the children on a trip around a school or home to find as many examples of ramps and wedges as you can. List, draw, or take photos of the examples you find. For more advanced work on simple machines, children can work with an adult to discuss and play the games at: www.edheads.org/activities/simple-machines.